Louisa Sherlock is dual qualified in dentistry and law. She practised as a dental surgeon for over a decade, both within the NHS and privately. As well as treating patients, she assisted with the running of a busy NHS practice and helped staff to prepare for CQC inspections.

Louisa carried out further training in the field of dentistry, completing a two-year diploma to become a member of the Joint Dental Faculties of the Royal College of Surgeons of England, London. Following a further qualification in aesthetic dentistry, Louisa developed a private practice involving cosmetic dentistry, invisible orthodontics and facial aesthetics. She also did some work for a nationwide facial aesthetics company. In addition, Louisa was a member of her Local Dental Committee for several years.

Throughout her legal training, Louisa received numerous awards, including the Lord Denning scholarship from Lincoln's Inn.

Louisa was called to the Bar in 2018 and is a member of No5 Chambers based in Birmingham and London. Most of her work is in the field of clinical negligence and personal injury. She regularly provides lectures to dental surgeons and experts on relevant legal matters as part of their Continuing Professional Development, and cross-examines experts as part of their assessments with the Expert Witness Institute.

A Practical Guide to Dental Negligence Litigation

A Practical Guide to Dental Negligence Litigation

Louisa Sherlock,
Barrister-at-Law,
BDS MJDF RCS (Eng)

Law Brief Publishing

Published 2023 by Law Brief Publishing, an imprint of Law Brief Publishing Ltd
30 The Parks
Minehead
Somerset
TA24 8BT

www.lawbriefpublishing.com

Paperback: 978-1-914608-68-1

For ISRS and DJNS.

Thank you for your love and support.

PREFACE

The aim of this book is to provide the reader with a practical guide to running a dental negligence case, whether that be for Claimant or Defendant.

This book is not intended to be a comprehensive guide on the subject of dentistry itself, but aims to provide the reader who is unfamiliar with reading dental records with a gentle introduction to the terminology used so that they can be more readily understood. With this understanding, the reader will be well placed to research further as necessary.

This book is also not intended to be a comprehensive guide to the law and procedure which one needs to know in order to successfully run a dental negligence claim. There is a vast amount of understanding of the law and procedure that one needs to have when one works in the field of clinical negligence, and this can be found in other texts. There is, in the writing of this book, a level of assumed knowledge on the part of the reader with regard to running clinical negligence cases, and the aim of this book is to provide advice and tips on matters that regularly crop up in dental negligence cases as separate from other clinical negligence matters.

The law as referenced is up to date at the time of writing (12 March 2023).

Louisa Sherlock
March 2023

CONTENTS

CHAPTER ONE

INTRODUCTION TO DENTISTRY

This chapter will provide an introduction to dental terminology because when working on dental negligence cases, having an understanding of the terminology used in dental records is helpful.

When a client approaches a solicitor with a potential dental negligence claim, the first step (after discussing the concerns that the client has about the treatment provided) will usually be to obtain the relevant dental records. For the lawyer who is new to dental negligence cases, dental records can at first seem impenetrable. Whilst it is neither necessary, nor possible, to describe in one book what is learned throughout the five-year dental degree course, this chapter aims to provide a gentle introduction to dental charting, firstly in order to aid with interpreting what has been recorded in the dental records, and also as a point of reference when reading expert reports.

Tooth Charting

When the dentist charts the patient's teeth, the mouth is divided into four quadrants (upper right, upper left, lower right and lower left). The deciduous (or milk/baby) teeth are the first teeth to erupt, and the teeth in each quadrant are labelled A-E, there being (usually) five teeth in each quadrant. The most anterior tooth, or the tooth closest to the front of the mouth and the midline in each quadrant, is A, and the most posterior tooth is E as follows:

EDCBA	ABCDE
EDCBA	ABCDE
(Right)	(Left)

When viewing this chart, imagine that the patient is facing you, so that the upper right A is that on the patient's upper right side, and therefore on the upper left quadrant of the chart.

Once the deciduous teeth exfoliate, they are replaced with permanent teeth. These are charted 1-8 in each quadrant as follows:

87654321	12345678
87654321	12345678

If a dentist is referring to the 1 in the upper right quadrant, they will call this tooth the upper right one, abbreviated to UR1. This is also known as the upper right central incisor.

The UR2 can also be referred to as the upper right lateral incisor.

The UR3 can also be referred to as the upper right canine.

The UR4 can also be referred to as the upper right first premolar, and the UR5 as the upper right second premolar.

The UR6 can also be referred to as the upper right first molar, the UR7 the upper right second molar, and the UR8 as the upper right third molar or upper right wisdom tooth.

Of course, the same terminology is applied across each quadrant.

An alternative way to notate the teeth is to give each quadrant a number: the upper right quadrant (permanent teeth) is 1, upper left 2, lower left 3 and lower right 4. The same pattern is followed for deciduous teeth where the upper right quadrant is 5, upper left 6, lower left 7 and lower right 8.

Thus, using this method of notation, upper right 1 is 11, and upper right A would be 5A. Lower left 4 would be 34, and the deciduous lower D would be 7D. Note, certain patients may have additional teeth to those usually found in the mouth, known as supernumerary teeth, and some patients will have missing teeth.

At each examination appointment, the dentist makes a record of all teeth which are present, all teeth which are missing, and all restorations on the teeth. That includes both direct restorations (fillings) and indirect restorations (those constructed in the lab, such as inlays, onlays, crowns and bridges). The dentist will also make a note of any implants present and any teeth which have been root treated (this is when the pulp tissue from inside the tooth has been removed, and a material is used to fill the internal cavity left behind). If the patient wears a denture, the dentist may make a note of this as well.

Periodontal Screening

In order to screen for periodontal disease, a dentist should also at every checkup appointment carry out what is known as a basic periodontal examination, or "BPE". This is where a dental instrument called a WHO BPE probe (World Health Organisation probe) is placed between the tooth and supporting gum to assess whether there is any loss of support, also known as pocketing. Depending on how healthy the gums are, a number is recorded, 0 being the most healthy and 4 being the least healthy. The highest score in the sextant is what will be noted.

The number recorded will help to determine a diagnosis with regard to gingival and periodontal health, and will also determine what treatment is required for the individual patient. Instead of the mouth being divided up into quadrants as it is for tooth charting, when charting the BPE, the mouth is divided into sextants, the upper right sextant being UR4-UR7, the upper central being UR3 – UL3 and the upper left sextant being UL4-UL7 (the lower sextants effectively mirror the uppers). All teeth are probed except the 8's.

A record should also be made of any furcations which are visible due to gum recession (typically marked with a "*"), bleeding on probing ("BOP"), any teeth which are mobile, and the Claimant's oral hygiene in general ("OH"). Should it be necessary, where there is a 3 or a 4, a dentist should then proceed to create a full periodontal chart (also known as six point probing), noting the measurements of six pockets around each tooth.

<u>Other Checks to be Carried Out</u>

An up-to-date medical history should be signed and dated at each appointment and any presenting complaints recorded.

A dentist should also routinely screen for oral cancer, occlusal wear and abrasion at each examination appointment. The health of the tempero-mandibular joint and soft tissues should be recorded, and any swollen lymph nodes noted.

Bitewing radiographs ("BWs") are usually taken at fairly regular intervals in order to assess patients for caries, pathology and to detect any horizontal bone loss which might be associated with periodontal disease. Further radiographs may be necessary depending on what is revealed on the bitewing radiographs, or what symptoms the patient presents with / what the dentists deems is necessary. All radiographs should be justified, that is, a reason provided for why they were taken, and a record should be made of what each radiograph reveals.

The dentist should decide what the caries and periodontal disease risk is for each patient (low/medium/high), and based on this, decide upon an appropriate recall interval (how frequently the patient should return for examinations).

Having carried out a full screening, the dentist also decides upon a diagnosis and a note of this should be made.

Treatment options should be discussed in detail with the patient in line with *Montgomery,* which will be discussed further in the chapter on Consent. The dentist and patient should then, together, create a treatment plan.

Once a treatment plan is created, a note of this is made. At future appointments, the dentist makes a detailed note of any treatment carried out, along with any complications, and what is to be done at the next appointment. The dentist should also make a note of any discussions which took place between themselves and the patient.

CHAPTER TWO

BREACH OF DUTY

It is well established in law that a dentist owes their patient a duty of care.

When considering whether a potential dental negligence claim has merit, the lawyer needs to know whether there has been a breach of that duty.

In order to find out whether there has been a breach of duty, an expert must be instructed to draft a report. When drafting this report, the expert is often also instructed to opine on causation (a topic covered in the next chapter).

Upon first receipt of a case, a lawyer may wish to consider instructing an expert to draft a brief screening report to assess whether this is a case which, at first glance, has good prospects of success. In an initial screening report, an expert will take a cursory look at the dental records and make a decision as to whether the case is worth investigating further. Should this report come back positive, then the lawyer can then instruct an expert to draft a more detailed breach and causation report.

It is important to know which expert to instruct to draft a breach of duty report. Lawyers running a dental negligence case need to instruct an expert who will know the standard of care and skill expected of the Defendant, or Defendants, in the case. There are numerous branches of dentistry as well as general dental practice; this will be considered further in the chapter "Which Expert to Instruct".

The requisite standard of care is primarily described in the case of *Bolam v Friern Hospital Management Committee* [1957] 1 W.L.R. 582. This is a very well-known case. However, the key points can sometimes be overlooked, and therefore they are set out below. See paragraph 586,

> "*...where you get a situation which involves the use of some special skill or competence, then the test as to whether there has been negligence or not is not the test of the man on the top of a Clapham omnibus, because he has not got this special skill. The test is the standard of the ordinary skilled man exercising and professing to have that special skill. A man need not possess the highest expert skill; it is well established law that it is sufficient if he exercises the ordinary skill of an ordinary competent man exercising that particular art.*"

Thus, take for example a case where it is alleged that there has been negligence on the part of a general dental surgeon. The standard expected of a general dental surgeon is that of a reasonably competent general dental surgeon.

Further, if the dentist can show that he/she acted in accordance with a competent body of professional opinion, this will be a defence to the claim, even if the body of opinion holding the contrary view is a minority one. See Bolam, paragraph 587,

> "*...if you are satisfied that they were acting in accordance with a practice of a competent body of professional opinion, then it would be wrong for you to hold that negligence was established.*"

Thus, as an example, in a claim against a general dental surgeon, a positive breach of duty report would establish that, on the balance of probabilities, the standard of care provided to the Claimant by the Defendant fell below that expected of a reasonably competent general dental surgeon, and no reasonable body of opinion would support any act or omission on the part of the Defendant.

Bolam was considered further in the case of *Bolitho v City and Hackney Health Authority* [1997] 3 WLR 1151 where it was decided, effectively, that as long as a competent reasonable body of professional opinion supports the way in which the healthcare professional carried out their work, and that opinion is not completely illogical, then the healthcare professional has not fallen below the standard expected of him / her. It was emphasised by Lord Browne-Wilkinson at page 243, paragraph C-D that it will "*seldom be right for a judge to reach the conclusion that views genuinely held by a competent medical expert are unreasonable…It is only where a judge can be satisfied that the body of expert opinion cannot be logically supported at all that such opinion will not provide the benchmark by reference to which the defendant's conduct falls to be assessed.*"

Following (*FB (Suing by her Mother and Litigation Friend, WAC) v Princess Alexandra Hospital NHS Trust* [2017] EWCA Civ 334), a dentist will be judged in accordance with the standard of reasonably competent practitioners of the same rank in the same discipline. Relevant youth and/or inexperience will not diminish nor increase the required standard.

See Lord Justice Jackson's comments at paragraph 63,

> "*The conduct of Dr Rushd in the present case must be judged by the standard of a reasonably competent SHO in an accident and emergency department. The fact that Dr Rushd was aged 25 and "relatively inexperienced"… does not diminish the required standard of skill and care. On the other hand, the fact that she had spent six months in a paediatric department does not elevate the required standard. Other SHOs in A&E departments will*

> *have different backgrounds and experience, but they are all judged by the same standard."*

Thus, a general dental practitioner who is newly qualified will be held to the same standard as a general dental practitioner with twenty or thirty years of experience. To look at the other side of the coin, a court won't expect more of a general dental practitioner with twenty or thirty years of experience; the standard expected will be that of a reasonably competent dental surgeon.

Furthermore, the standard of care expected doesn't differ between private and NHS work. However, a different standard of care might arguably be expected of a dentist working in a practice holding itself out as, for example, one of the country's leading implant providers.

Challenges lawyers often face when seeking to establish breach of duty in dental negligence cases

Challenges faced are as follows.

1. *Identifying breaches from the expert report*

It is always worth bearing in mind that an expert report may be drafted in such a way that breaches are contained partly within the chronology section and partly within the causation section. When first reading through a breach and causation report, a good starting point is to identify all the breaches which can be found throughout the report and to list them. Whether or not the breaches are causative can be considered at a later stage.

2. *Satisfying the legal test*

It is not uncommon for experts to draft an opinion on breach of duty and state that there has been a breach of duty because they personally would not have carried out treatment in such a way, or a reasonable body of opinion would support carrying out treatment in a different way. This, of course, is not the legal test, and at times it is necessary to challenge the expert as to, in the case of a general dental surgeon, whether it is their opinion that the standard of care fell below that of a reasonably competent general dental surgeon, and that no reasonable body of opinion would support the act or omission of the Defendant. If the Claimant's expert cannot go so far as to satisfy the test on any given potential breach, then that breach naturally falls away. If acting for the Defendant, and the expert says that a reasonable body of professional opinion would support the act or omission of the Defendant, then that allegation of breach of duty can reasonably be defended.

3. *Inherent risks of treatment*

There are some potential breaches of duty that typically arise in dental negligence cases which may, in fact, be inherent risks of treatment. Two examples are a fracturing a file in the process of carrying out root canal therapy, or creating a pulpal exposure when preparing a tooth for a filling.

Whilst carrying out root canal therapy, a dentist uses what are known as files to remove nerve tissue. On occasion, a file can fracture in the process, and this is an inherent risk of root canal therapy. However, it can also occur as a result of failing to properly utilise the file. An example would be a case where a dentist has not used lubrication whilst filing. Further, in cases where the dentist has used the file correctly with lubrication, and has therefore not breached their duty of care in that regard, they may have failed to advise the patient that the file has fractured only for the patient to be informed at a later date, perhaps when they experience pain or attend an appointment with another dentist. This failure to advise of the file fracture and manage the situation appropriately would then constitute a breach of duty.

With the example of pulpal exposure, exposing nerve tissue within a tooth (by drilling into the pulpal cavity when using a handpiece to remove caries) which then results in loss of vitality of the tooth is an inherent risk of cavity preparation. However, it may be the case that pre-operative radiographs reveal that the caries was superficial, and therefore on the balance of probabilities, an exposure was as a result of a breach of duty.

These are examples where the possibility of establishing that a breach of duty has occurred requires careful thought. These examples of potential breaches are not clear-cut, but at the same time, they should not be written off as inherent risks of treatment before they have been properly considered.

4. Consent

This can prove to be a thorny issue; see the chapter on Consent for further consideration of the topic.

5. Breaches which are not properly particularised in the expert report

It is important to ensure that all breaches are sufficiently detailed so that the Defendant will be able to fully consider the case and respond. As an example, an expert may say that a thorough or proper examination was not carried out by the Defendant at any stage. However, if this were to be put to a Defendant in a Letter of Claim or Particulars of Claim, the Defendant is likely to simply not respond and say that the allegation is not properly particularised. What is required is for the expert to say what they would have expected from a reasonably competent general dental surgeon when carrying out an examination (what checks should have been carried out, and what should have been recorded), and how frequently such an examination ought to have been carried out.

Another example is where a dentist has carried out root canal therapy, and it is the expert's view that this has not been carried out to a reasonable standard. It would not be sufficient for an expert to simply make a bald statement to that effect. What would be required would be for the expert to say why specifically the root canal therapy fell below the standard expected, for example, because the obturation material was short of the apex (the tip of the root), or not properly condensed. This may need to be drawn out of the expert either through written questions or in conference.

6. *Missed breaches of duty*

An expert may fail to consider a breach which is in fact relevant and causative. At times this may be because it seems so obvious to them that they simply have not written it down, or it may be that it is something they have not yet considered. Further, given that the condition and prognosis ("C&P") report is usually drafted after the breach and causation report, there can, on occasion, be something which arises following examination of the Claimant for the purposes of producing the C&P report which an expert then needs to consider as part of their breach report, ie, did any breaches on the part of the Defendant cause this loss?

7. *Breaches of duty which occur over many years*

There are cases where a patient's dental health has been neglected over many years, sometimes over decades. It is then necessary to go through the records and identify each breach and the date on which it occurred. An example would be where a dentist has failed to carry out BPE scoring regularly. A note should be made of each appointment when this was not done when the Claimant says it ought to have been done.

There are also cases where an expert will focus on a specific period of time, and not consider the case as a whole, and it is then necessary to assess the case further, either through written questions or in conference.

8. Multiple Defendants

Where the alleged breaches occurred over many years and the patient has been treated by more than one dentist in this time, for example, due to attending more than one dentist in the practice and/or having been referred to other dental practitioners, it is important to consider which breaches occurred on the part of each Defendant, and list these clearly.

9. Poor dental record keeping

Whilst poor record keeping can be a breach of duty in its own right, it can be difficult to establish clearly whether there has been a breach of duty on the part of a Defendant where the standard of record keeping is so poor that an expert struggles to work out what has happened. Poor record keeping can be indicative of a poor standard of care generally on the part of the Defendant, but where it is difficult to work out what treatment was done and on what dates, it can take time to decipher the records and set out a clear case in respect of breach of duty.

CHAPTER THREE

CAUSATION

To establish causation, the Claimant must prove that on the balance of probabilities, the Defendant's breach or breaches of duty caused injury.

The standard "but for" test usually applies, see *Fairchild v Glenhaven* [2002] UKHL 22, where Lord Bingham summaries the test,

> "*In the generality of personal injury actions, it is of course true that the claimant is required to discharge the burden of showing that the breach of which he complains caused the damage for which he claims and to do so by showing that but for the breach he would not have suffered the damage.*"

If the "but for" test cannot be satisfied, then consider whether any alleged breach materially (ie more than minimally) contributed to the Claimant's injury. See below for further discussion on this.

A good starting point is to go through the breaches that have been identified and listed, and work out which, if any, caused the Claimant injury. Causation points should be set out in the causation section of the expert's report, but again, don't necessarily expect to find such points only within the causation section. They may be interspersed within the chronology, breach sections, or even within the summary or conclusion.

In some cases, causation may be relatively straightforward to prove, such as where the dentist extracted the wrong tooth, and this breach of duty therefore clearly caused the loss of the tooth.

In other cases, it is not so straightforward to establish causation, for example, where a tooth which was lost had a questionable prognosis in any event. In this example, it may be the case that causation is not made out, it may be that the alleged breach materially contributed to the loss, or it may be that the alleged breach accelerated the loss (in which case it might be necessary to tease out in written questions to the expert or in conference when, on balance, the loss would have occurred but for the breach).

Once causation has been fully explored, any breaches which are not causative can be disregarded and should not be pleaded in the Letter of Claim, nor in the Particulars of Claim.

Difficulties often encountered in dental negligence claims when trying to establish causation

1. Multiple Defendants

Where a Claimant has been treated by more than one dentist, and particularly when this has taken place over a period of many years, it can be difficult to work out what breaches, and therefore which dentist, caused the identified injuries.

Whilst the breaches and causation points can, at times, be readily separated out with careful analysis, there are cases where they cannot because the breaches of more than one dentist have caused a particular injury. When this occurs, it is necessary to consider whether the breaches of more than one Defendant appear to have caused injury, and whether therefore both or more Defendants are jointly and severally liable for the injury.

2. *Material contribution*

It may be the case that a Defendant's breach of duty is not the sole cause of the Claimant's injury, but that it materially contributed to the injury. There is a plethora of case law on the topic of material contribution, the law has become incredibly complex and rather confused due to differing uses of the terms "divisible", "indivisible" and "cumulative" and it is beyond the scope of this book to consider the topic in full, but a few relevant points are set out below.

Where the injury is divisible in the sense that its progression and severity is dose-dependent, or driven by exposure, such as profound hypoxic ischaemia, (as opposed to an all or nothing indivisible injury where one either has it or one does not, such as cancer or a broken bone), a starting point is that a Defendant will be liable only for the proportion resulting from their negligence if medical science and expert evidence can establish what this proportion is.

See, though, the recent recent High Court Judgment in *CNZ v Royal Bath Hospitals NHS Foundation* [2023] EWHC 19 (KB) where the Claimant developed cerebral palsy as a result of acute profound hypoxic ischaemia ("PHI"). Mr Justice Ritchie found that the injury was divisible because brain damage due to PHI does not grow like cancer or mesothelioma once triggered. Instead, the spread of damage due to PHI is dose dependent, and the more PHI the foetus suffers, the greater the brain damage. Further, there was only one cause of injury, the PHI. Mr Justice Ritchie stated that if the "but for" test was not made out on his calculations, and there was some non-negligent PHI, then given that it was impossible and not merely difficult to quantify the functional outcome for each minute of negligently caused acute PHI, and so long as the Claimant could prove that the breach made a material contribution to the reduced functional outcome which was more than de-minimis, the Claimant could recover 100% of the damages.

With an indivisible injury, it is suggested in *Bailey v Ministry of Defence* [2008] EWCA Civ 883 and *Williams v Bermuda Hospitals Boards* [2016] UKPC 4 that where it is found that the breach of a Defendant caused or contributed to the Claimant's injury, then even though there may have been other contributing causes, the Defendant will be held fully liable for it. See the following quote from paragraph 46 of Bailey as stated by Lord Justice Waller with whom Lord Justice Sedley and Lady Justice Smith agreed,

> "*If the evidence demonstrates on a balance of probabilities that the injury would have occurred as a result of the non-tortious cause or causes in any event, the claimant will have failed to establish that the tortious cause contributed. Hotson exemplifies such a situation. If the evidence demonstrates that 'but for' the contribution of the tortious cause the injury would probably not have occurred, the claimant will (obviously) have discharged the burden. In a case where medical science cannot establish the probability that 'but for' an act of negligence the injury would not have happened but can establish that the contribution of the negligent cause was more than negligible, the 'but for' test is modified, and the claimant will succeed.*"

If it cannot be said that the breach caused or contributed to the injury but is simply a possible cause among other possible causes, then the claim will fail, *Wilsher v Essex Area Health Authority [1988]* AC 1074. Further, if the breach of duty has only contributed to the risk of injury, and not the injury itself, then the claim will fail, *Ministry of Defence v AB* [2010] EWCA Civ 1317."

However, note that in *Thorley v Sandwell and West Birmingham Hospitals NHS Trust* [2021] EWHC 2604 (QB), Mr Justice Soole considered the case of *AB* to be "*binding authority that the test of material contribution has no application to a case where there is indivisible injury and one tortfeasor*" (paragraph 147) and stated that the legal issue is "*ripe for authoritative review*", (paragraph 151).

Clearly the law is highly complex in this area, and therefore careful thought must be given to the circumstances of the case and whether material contribution applies before pleading it.

3. Poorly maintained dentition

When a Claimant has attended a dentist for treatment, and at the outset they had a poorly maintained / heavily diseased dentition, it can be difficult to ascertain whether a loss is attributable to a breach. For example, if a Claimant has attended with extensive caries, and then had restorative work on a tooth that failed, it can be difficult to establish whether the work failed because it was substandard as opposed to the fact that the tooth was badly damaged before treatment commenced. An expert may not have considered this at the outset, and this is when it is necessary to explore the point fully in conference or by way of written questions.

There are cases where a Defendant will attempt to argue simply that a tooth was not restorable and that is why the restoration failed, but this is not necessarily a good argument to raise as it begs the question as to why the Defendant did indeed choose to restore an unrestorable tooth.

4. Periodontal disease

There can be a variety of factors which contribute to periodontal disease. These include the patient's own host response (how their immune system responds to bacteria which are present in the mouth), their oral hygiene levels and smoking. A treating dentist has a duty to diagnose periodontal disease, advise the Claimant that they have the disease, manage the disease through regular professional cleaning and tailored oral hygiene instruction, and also to monitor the progression of the disease. However, due to the numerous factors which come together in causing or contributing to periodontal disease, and which impact on how a particular patient responds to treatment, it can be difficult to properly establish causation in respect of any alleged breaches on the part of a Defendant. In such cases, it can be helpful to instruct a periodontist to opine on the very discrete issue of causation in relation to periodontal disease, that is, whether the progression of the Claimant's periodontal disease has been caused by any breach on the part of the Defendant, and if so, to what extent the disease has progressed as a result of any such breach. See also the above section on material contribution.

5. *Irregular attenders*

Where a Claimant has failed to attend their dentist regularly, it can prove difficult to establish causation. Whilst this may not be so much of an issue where the breaches occurred over a discrete period of time throughout which the Claimant did attend for treatment, it can be more difficult where the alleged breaches stretch over a long period of time. If, for example, a Claimant is seeking to establish that negligence over many years led to the loss of their teeth, but when looking through the records there are many appointments over the years where the Claimant has failed to attend or failed to return for further treatment, it can be difficult to prove that the loss is as a result of the Defendant's negligence and not as a result of the Claimant's irregular attendance.

An example is where a Claimant is seeking to establish that periodontal disease has resulted from the Defendant's failure to properly diagnose and treat their periodontal disease. The management of periodontal disease requires regular treatment from the treating dentist, as well as motivation on the part of the patient to maintain adequate oral hygiene and not smoke. Whilst in many cases, a Defendant will argue that there is an element of contributory negligence on the part of the Claimant in any event in that periodontal disease does not typically present where a patient maintains good oral hygiene, there may be some cases where the Claimant is such an irregular attender that it is not possible to link any breaches on the part of the Defendant to the progression of periodontal disease. See also the above section on material contribution.

6. *Poor dental record keeping*

As with establishing breach, it can be difficult to establish causation when the standard of record keeping is so poor that it is difficult to work out what treatment was carried out and when. Such cases may require additional thought and careful consideration.

7. *Consent*

Causation can be difficult to prove in consent cases because it is necessary to prove that had the correct consent process taken place, the Claimant would have opted for a different treatment option or would have deferred treatment. The case can then become a factual dispute where, should the case run to trial, the outcome may depend largely upon how the Claimant comes across a trial (see the Chapter on "consent" for further detail). See *Malik v St George's University Hospitals* NHSFT [2021] EWHC 1913 (QB) as an example of a case where the judge was not persuaded by the Claimant that on the balance of probabilities, had alternative options been explained to him, he would have declined the offer of surgery, nor that he would have sought another opinion or delayed making his decision (this was said *obiter* given that the Claimant failed to establish breach of duty in any event, appeal pending).

Further, note that in *CNZ,* Mr Justice Ritchie considered that *Montgomery* probably did apply in 1996, but doubted that it could be taken as far back as the 1950s or 1960s.

TOP TIPS ON BREACH OF DUTY AND CAUSATION

From experience of dental negligence claims, here are a few matters which arise on a fairly regular basis:

- It may be that there are a few steps involved when considering the issue of causation. For example, if the expert says that a Claimant should have been referred to hospital for treatment, and it was a breach of duty to fail to refer, then what needs to be considered is what should have happened if the Claimant had been referred to hospital. On balance, would having treatment carried out in hospital have prevented the loss from occurring, or was there a significant risk that the loss would have occurred in any event?

- Another example is where a Claimant suffered a nerve injury following a lower wisdom tooth extraction. In this example, the expert says that a radiograph ought to have been taken before attempting extraction, and the failure to take a radiograph before extracting the tooth was a breach of duty. It would then be necessary to consider what that radiograph would have shown, and what should have happened next. If it is the expert's opinion that the radiograph would have revealed that the roots of the wisdom tooth were in close proximity to the lower inferior alveolar nerve, then it is likely that the Claimant ought to have been referred into hospital for an oral surgeon to carry out the extraction. The expert will then need to consider whether, on the balance of probabilities, the Claimant would not have suffered the nerve injury had an oral surgeon carried out the extraction. However, if the radiograph would have revealed that this was an extraction which could reasonably have been carried out in general practice, then it may be the case that no causation flows from the breach (subject to consideration of the case of *Chester* which is discussed further in the chapter on Consent).

- A breach which experts tend to identify quite regularly when it comes to root canal therapy is the failure of a dentist to use a rubber dam when carrying out treatment. This can lead to ingress of bacteria when carrying out the treatment, but it may be difficult to prove, on the balance of probabilities, that it was this failing that ultimately led to the failure of the root canal therapy, and therefore careful thought needs to be given as to whether this ought to be pleaded.

- Experts quite regularly identify poor record keeping as being a breach of duty. However, in many cases this is not necessarily causative. An example of where it may be causative is where it can be argued that but for the failure to maintain adequate records, the treating dentist or future dentist/s would have recognised the need for particular follow-up care which would have, in turn, prevented a loss. Thought needs to be given as to whether this is a causative breach in the circumstances.

Next Steps

Should the breach and causation report come back positive, then a solicitor acting for the Claimant should at this stage consider getting counsel on board to assess prospects, preferably counsel who has experience in dental negligence claims. Dental negligence claims can span a significant period of time in that negligence may have occurred over many years, sometimes involving several dentists or dental professionals. Experienced counsel will consider the report and, with a conference if necessary, form a view as to prospects. Counsel can advise as to whether this is a case which should be run on a Conditional Fee Agreement ("CFA") basis, and if so, against which potential Defendant or Defendants. Depending on the complexity of the case and experience level of the solicitor conducting the case, counsel's opinion as to prospects and next steps at this stage is likely to help streamline a case and save costs in the long run.

If acting for the Defendant, obtaining a breach and causation report should enable proper consideration of the merits of the case, and assist with the drafting of a Letter of Response. The above comments with regard to getting experienced counsel on board at this stage also apply.

CHAPTER FOUR

CONTRIBUTORY NEGLIGENCE

A Defendant will often need to consider whether it is appropriate to raise an allegation of contributory negligence, particularly in cases where there is alleged negligence over a period of many years, and where there is evidence that the Claimant has a heavily restored dentition, frequently presents with dental caries and / or has periodontal disease. This is because dental caries typically develops when a patient has a diet which is high in sugar, and periodontal disease typically develops when a patient has suboptimal oral hygiene, and also in smokers.

The likelihood of success of such an argument is dependent on many factors, in particular the following:

i) how regularly the Claimant attended their dentist, in particular, over the material time. A Claimant who is a regular attender is more likely to be able to effectively counter such an allegation in demonstrating that they did take responsibility for their own dental health in attending appointments regularly, and argue that they entrusted the care of their oral health to the treating dentist. In contrast, it is difficult to show that an irregular attender is actively taking responsibility for their oral health, particularly if they have been advised of the need to attend regularly, and there is evidence in the notes that such advice has been given;

ii) whether there is any evidence of preventative advice having been given. Where there is a record of a dentist having given a

Claimant advice repeatedly, such as dietary advice, smoking cessation advice, and / or tailored oral hygiene advice, and there is evidence that the Claimant has failed to heed this advice, an allegation of contributory negligence is more likely to succeed. Where no preventative advice has been given, it can be more difficult for a Defendant to argue successfully that a Claimant ought to have taken better care of their own oral health if the Claimant has entrusted their care to a dentist, and the dentist has not advised them of the same.

CHAPTER FIVE

CONSENT

Consent is an area which requires careful consideration because it often crops up in dental negligence cases.

An example is where the Claimant states that they were not fully informed of the risks of treatment that they underwent, and/or that they were not advised of alternative treatment options, and if they had been so advised, they would not have opted to go ahead with the treatment that the Defendant then provided.

When considering consent in dental negligence cases, if the Claimant alleges breach of duty, it is important that the expert, in their report, clearly sets out the risks of treatment which should have been explained to the Claimant, the treatment alternatives which should have been provided, and the risks and benefits of those treatment alternatives. It is then for the Claimant to say what he or she would have decided to do had this information been provided to them before treatment. Clearly the Claimant now has the benefit of hindsight, but they must try to put themselves in the position they were in before the treatment was carried out. Should the Defendant argue that the Claimant would have gone ahead with treatment in any event, then the case becomes a factual dispute as to whether any breach is causative, potentially taking into account records of any previous discussions which have taken place between the Claimant and Defendant.

The key case to consider is that of *Montgomery v Lanarkshire Health Board* [2015] UKSC 11. In this case, as a result of complications during delivery, the Claimant's baby was born with severe disabilities.

It was the Claimant's case that she ought to have been warned about the increased risk of mechanical difficulties during brith, specifically shoulder dystocia, given that she suffered from insulin dependent diabetes mellitus and was carrying a larger than normal baby. She said she should have been offered the alternative possibility of delivery by elective caesarean section. It was stated at paragraph 87 by Lord Kerr and Lord Reed (with whom Lord Neuberger, Lord Clarke, Lord Wilson and Lord Hodge agreed),

"The doctor is therefore under a duty to take reasonable care to ensure that the patient is aware of any material risks involved in any recommended treatment, and of any reasonable alternative or variant treatments. The test of materiality is whether, in the circumstances of the particular case, a reasonable person in the patient's position would be likely to attach significance to the risk, or the doctor is or should reasonably be aware that the particular patient would be likely to attach significance to it."

The assessment as to whether a risk is material or not is fact-sensitive and sensitive to the characteristics of the particular patient; it can't be reduced merely to percentages (see paragraph 89). The significance of a given risk is likely to reflect "*for example, the nature of the risk, the effect which its occurrence would have upon the life of the patient, the importance to the patient of the benefits sought to be achieved by the treatment, the alternatives, and the risks involved in those alternatives*" [paragraph 89].

Further, in order to discharge the duty of care, the information must be provided to the patient in such a way that a patient can understand it – a medical professional won't discharge his/her duty of care if he/she bombards the patient with technical information that the patient couldn't be expected to grasp. Further, consent won't be obtained simply by signing a routine consent form (see paragraph 90).

Montgomery provides for the fact that a patient can decide that he or she does not wish to be informed of risks of injury, and in these situations, a health practitioner would not be obliged to discuss the risks inherent in treatment with a person who makes it clear that they would prefer not to discuss the matter (see paragraph 85).

The judgment in *Montgomery* took into account social and legal developments which point away from a doctor-patient relationship based upon medical paternalism, and made it clear that their Lordships had in their mind that a development in the way in which healthcare services are provided is that patients are "*now widely regarded as persons holding rights, rather than as the passive recipients of the care of the medical profession. They are also widely treated as consumers exercising choices…*" (paragraph 75). Their Lordships made clear in paragraph 75 that they intended the judgment to be relevant not only to doctors, but to other healthcare providers (thus, the judgment is relevant to dental negligence cases). They also note in the judgement that they intend a movement away from *Bolam* when considering the issue of consent,

> "*It follows that the analysis of the law by the majority in Sidaway is unsatisfactory, in so far as it treated the doctor's duty to advise her patient of the risks of proposed treatment as falling within the scope of the Bolam test…There is no reason to perpetuate the application of the Bolam test in this context any longer*" (paragraph 86).

A relatively recent case in the High Court in 2021, *Malik v St George's University Hospitals NHSFT* [2021] EWHC 1913 (QB), applies *Montgomery*. Appeal is, at the time of writing, pending.

Malik involves a claim following further spinal surgery which ultimately worsened rather than improved the Claimant's condition. The Claimant had initially underwent a laminectomy and discectomy to decompress the spinal cord at T10/T11 where it was severely compressed. Healing was slow and incomplete: the Claimant had suffered neurological damage and experienced ongoing numbness and weakness of his left leg.

The Defendant advised that further surgery ought be undertaken at two sites, namely: (i) a revision thoracic decompression of the exiting nerve root on the left hand side at T10/T11; and (ii) a lumbar decompression at L3/L4. The Defendant filled out some paperwork that day in order to put the Claimant on his waiting list for an urgent operation to those areas, and the surgery took place a month later. Whilst there was no criticism about the quality of the Defendant's surgery, nor the post-operative care provided, very regrettably the outcome for the Claimant was to render him very significantly worse off than he had been before, confining him for the most part to life in a wheelchair.

It was the Claimant's case that he did not give his informed consent to revision surgery.

His Honour Judge Blair QC identified the following issues in the case at paragraph 18:

> "*i) was the claimant complaining of terrible intercostal pain on 13 July 2015 when he visited Mr Minhas' clinic?*
>
> *ii) if he was, how long had he been suffering from it?*
>
> *iii) if he was, would a responsible body of competent and reasonable neurosurgeons have concluded that a significant proportion of that pain was radicular in nature and caused by compression to the left sided T10/T11 nerve root?*
>
> *iv) if so, would a responsible body of competent and reasonable neurosurgeons have offered revision surgery at that location*

in the light of its reasonably and competently assessed potential benefits and risks?

v) even if they would, were there reasonable alternatives to surgery which, in the light of their respective benefits and risks, no responsible and reasonably competent neurosurgeon would have omitted to offer to the claimant?

vi) was the offer of surgery (and, if established, any reasonable alternatives which should have been offered) adequately explained to the claimant in terms of its benefits and risks so as to obtain his informed consent to the surgery performed?

vii) if a breach of duty has been proved on the balance of probabilities, applying the appropriate legal test, has the claimant also established that the negligence caused his injury and loss?"

The Claimant's expert, Mr Todd, a consultant neurosurgeon and spinal surgeon, stated at paragraph 72 that there were reasonable alternatives to surgery which "*no responsible and reasonably competent neurosurgeon would have omitted to offer to the Claiman*t." These included:

i) injections of steroids / local anaesthetic to the nerve root, both as a diagnostic tool but also to relieve pain;

ii) the greater use of analgesia whilst waiting to see if things improved;

iii) a pain management strategy.

The Claimant said that had he been informed of alternative treatments, and had he been told properly of the risks of the surgery and the scale of its potential benefits, he would have chosen an alternative in preference to surgery.

The Defendant's expert, Mr Ivanov, a consultant neurosurgeon and spinal surgeon accepted that some spinal surgeons would try an injection first, however another "*perfectly reasonable group*" would consider this to be causing an unnecessary delay to treatment when a calcified disc compression will persist (see paragraph 77).

Mr Ivanov also stated he considered it questionable as to whether it was logical in the above circumstances to mention spinal injections to the patient, although he accepted that some surgeons would consider it good practice (paragraph 78).

The judge, however, did not find that the Defendant was obliged to advise the patient of this alternative treatment because he found that "*a responsible, competent and respectable body of skilled spinal surgeons would have reasonably concluded that there were no reasonable alternative treatments available in the context of the parameters and discussion that the Claimant had with Mr Minhas*".

The judge made it clear that if he had been persuaded that there had been a breach of duty, then any breaches would not have caused the injuries which the Claimant has suffered. Had the option of an injection or any other options been explained to him, then with Mr Minhas's respectable opinions as to their respective risks and chances of providing any desired benefit, he found that the Claimant would not have declined nor postponed the offer of surgery.

The wording of the judge's reasoning in *Malik* does appear to introduce an element of *Bolam* to the test as set out in *Montgomery* in that the judge considered what a responsible, competent and respectable body of professional opinion would consider to be a reasonable treatment option when deciding what alternative treatments ought to have been provided to the Claimant, and it will be interesting to see the outcome of the appeal.

Another case which it is important to bear in mind, and which sometimes needs consideration in dental negligence consent cases, is that of *Chester v Afshar* [2004] UKHL 41. In this case, the Claimant was not warned about a small (1-2%) but unavoidable risk that the proposed operation may result in serious neurological damage. The surgery did, although skilfully performed, lead to the Claimant developing serious neurological damage. The Claimant admitted that she would still have gone ahead with surgery if warned of this risk, but she would have sought further advice on alternatives, and therefore the operation would not have taken place when it did. The risk of the Claimant suffering serious neurological damage as a result would have been the same, ie 1-2%, and therefore it was found that it was improbable that she would have sustained the neurological damage had the surgery been performed on a different day. Consequently, the Claimant established a causal link between the breach and the injury sustained, and the Defendant was liable in damages.

This decision of the trial judge was upheld in the Court of Appeal and the House of Lords, Lord Bingham of Cornhill and Lord Hoffmann dissenting.

Lord Bingham of Cornhill, in his dissenting judgment, stated at paragraph 9 that to allow the Claimant to succeed would be a "*substantial and unjustified departure from sound and established principles*" and the that the timing of the operation was irrelevant to the injury the Claimant suffered because, "*That injury would have been as liable to occur whenever the surgery was performed and whoever performed it*" (paragraph 8).

Lord Hoffmann, in his dissenting judgment, stated that in his opinion, the argument that the Defendant's breach of duty caused the

Claimant's injury was as logical as saying that "*if one had been told, on entering a casino, that the odds on No7 coming up at roulette were only 1 in 37, one would have gone away and come back next week or gone to a different casino.*" (Paragraph 31). He said that the trial judge had found as a fact that the risk of the Claimant developing neurological damage would have been precisely the same if she had the surgery at another time or by another surgeon, and that it therefore follows that the Claimant failed to prove that the breach of duty caused her loss, and that on ordinary principles of tort law, the Defendant was not liable.

However, Lord Steyn (Lord Hope of Craighead and Lord Walker of Gestingthorpe assenting) makes it clear in his judgment that this decision reflects a need to maintain the autonomy and dignity of each patient in cases where they have not given informed consent, and that the only time that a medical professional does not owe a legal duty to a patient to warn him or her of possible serious risks is in a wholly exceptional case where objectively it is in in the best interests of the patient. It is stated that the aspiration of the law is to right wrongs, and that the decision reflects the reasonable expectations of the public in contemporary society. Their Lordships rely upon this to justify what is described as "*a narrow and modest departure from traditional causation principles*" (paragraph 24) and that "*a claimant ought not to be without a remedy, even if it involves some extension of existing principle*" (paragraph 101).

Thus, if the Defendant fails to warn of a small but recognisable risk of a particular condition arising as a result of dental surgery, and the Claimant goes on to suffer from that condition, then if it is not argued that the Claimant would not have gone ahead with surgery but would instead have postponed treatment whilst obtaining further information, then it can be argued that, applying *Chester*, on the balance of probabilities, the breach caused the loss.

There has, however, been some recent judicial criticism of the reasoning in *Chester.* See, for example, the Court of Appeal case of *Duce v Worcestershire Acute Hospitals NHS Trust* [2018] EWCA Civ 1307. Lord Justice Leggatt described the decision in *Chester* as being problematic, and stated that the right to make an informed choice was not a right traditionally protected by the tort of negligence. It was stated that whilst there was a reluctance in *Chester* to deprive an honest claimant of a remedy where they admitted that if the risk was explained to them, they would not have declined surgery once and for all, this concern actually related to difficulty in the proof of causation (paragraph 90). Further, "*These are all matters which may be thought ripe for the Supreme Court when the opportunity arises*" (paragraph 92). However, in *Duce,* this did not assist the Claimant because here it was found as a fact that, had she been warned of the risk, the Claimant would still have proceeded with the operation as and when she did.

It was noted by Lord Justice Hamblen in paragraph 70 that if "*the exceptional principle of causation*" established in Chester is to be relied upon, it is necessary to plead it and prove that, if warned by the risk, the Claimant would have deferred the operation.

Thus, if relying upon the principle established in *Chester,* it is necessary to fully plead it in the Particulars of Claim, and also to bear in mind that the decision may be ripe for reconsideration should an appeal reach the Supreme Court.

CHAPTER SIX

EXPERT EVIDENCE – WHICH EXPERT TO INSTRUCT

There are several branches of dentistry outside of general dental practice, including the following:

- endodontics (root canal therapy);
- periodontics (the management of gum disease);
- prosthodontics (replacement of missing teeth or restoration of teeth with indirect materials, ie restorations made in a dental laboratory) ;
- restorative dentistry (the restoration of carious or damaged teeth);
- orthodontics (straightening teeth);
- paedodontics (management of children's dental health);
- oral surgery (extraction of teeth and surgical procedures carried out within the mouth);
- maxillofacial surgery (surgery carried out due to disease, trauma, injuries and defects to the face);
- implantology (the placement and maintenance of implants);

- cosmetic / aesthetic dentistry (dentistry which is carried out to improve the physical appearance of the patient's dentition. This may include facial aesthetics, that is, wrinkle reducing injections and dermal fillers).

Chapter Two considers the standard of care required.

With that in mind, when considering breach of duty, it is important to try to instruct an expert who is in the same position or role as the Defendant. For example, if the Defendant is a general dental surgeon, then a general dental surgeon ought to be instructed to opine on breach of duty. If the Defendant is a consultant oral surgeon, then a consultant oral surgeon ought to be instructed to opine on breach. This is because they will be the right person to speak as to the standard of care expected of a reasonably competent practitioner of the same rank and discipline, and therefore whether there has been a breach of that duty. Should the expert for the Claimant and the expert for the Defendant differ in their opinion on breach of duty, then the court is likely to prefer the opinion of an expert who is of the same rank and discipline as the Defendant because a judge would probably consider them to be more likely to appreciate, through experience, what the standard of care expected of the Defendant would be.

When it comes to the issue of causation, it may be that a different expert to the breach expert needs to be instructed, at least to opine on particular aspects of the case. For example, if the Defendant is a general dental surgeon, then whilst a general dental surgeon would be the correct expert to opine on breach of duty in terms of diagnosing and managing periodontal disease in general practice, a general dental surgeon would be unlikely to be able to comment on what, if any, loss was caused by this breach of duty.

In certain circumstances, it may be necessary to instruct an endodontist to opine on causation, for example, if a general dentist is unsure as to when, on the balance of probabilities, loss of vitality of a tooth occurred, and therefore whether any loss flows from the breach.

Some thought also needs to be given as to which expert ought to be instructed to draft a condition and prognosis report. For example, if the Claimant seeks implants to replace their missing teeth, then ideally an implantologist or a dentist who places implants should be instructed. Only an expert with this practical experience should be opining as to the suitability of the Claimant for implants, creating an appropriate treatment plan, and setting out how much it will cost to place and maintain the implants and their respective crowns or abutments.

Dental expert reports can be very expensive to obtain, and it is therefore worth thinking very carefully, before instructing an expert, about whether they are the right person to draft the report. Experienced counsel and/or experienced dental experts should be able to help provide a guide as to which field an expert ought to be instructed from if necessary.

TOP TIPS

When deciding which expert to instruct to assess the standard of care, and whether there has been a breach of duty, a good starting point would be to find out what position the Defendant holds, and instruct an expert at the same level. For example, if this is a case about a general dental practitioner who has failed to properly diagnose and treat gum disease, then the right expert to instruct to assess breach would be a general dental practitioner as opposed to a specialist periodontist where a different standard of care would be expected.

- Remember to consider whether it is necessary, based on the information provided by the Claimant, to instruct a psychologist or psychiatrist to draft a report. There are times where the alleged negligence has severely affected a Claimant psychologically, and it is important to be alive to this.

- In an orthodontics case, consider whether orthodontics has been provided by a specialist orthodontist or consultant orthodontist, or whether "invisible orthodontics" has been provided by a general dental surgeon. This will help to determine which expert to instruct when considering breach of duty.

CHAPTER SEVEN

QUANTUM

Anticipated treatment costs are typically provided within the condition and prognosis report, although the breach and causation expert may also provide proposed figures in their report. Where the reports are drafted by two different experts and differ, it is important to clarify the figures before the Schedule of Loss is sent to the Defendant.

It is also necessary to go through the anticipated treatment costs and make sure that these do indeed flow from the alleged negligence. For example, treatment costs for periodontal treatment are often included in a condition and prognosis report. In a case where the allegation is that the Defendant failed to properly diagnose and treat the Claimant's periodontal disease, then treatment for periodontal disease would likely have been required in any event at the point where the Defendant should have diagnosed it as being present. It might be the case that more extensive periodontal treatment is now required because of alleged breaches, at least at the outset or for a certain period of time, but that is not the same as claiming periodontal treatment for the rest of the Claimant's life where this may well have been required in any event.

When drafting the Schedule of Loss, consider the following:

1. Past Losses

Within this section will be:

i) the cost of reasonable remedial treatment which has already taken place and which was required as a result of the alleged negligence;

ii) the cost of any unnecessary treatment carried out by the Defendant, for example, if the Claimant attended appointments relating to pain where this was not properly addressed, or crowns that failed within a very short space of time and were replaced several times;

iii) mileage for such appointments;

iv) any loss of earnings as a result of needing to take time off due to pain as a consequence of the alleged negligence, or as a result of having to attend unnecessary appointments or appointments for treatment to remedy the losses flowing from the alleged negligence;

v) the cost of any prescriptions or painkillers reasonably required as a result of the alleged negligence. A reasonable figure can be claimed, even in the absence of evidence (see for example the first instance judgment of Leveson J in *Hesp v Willemse* [2002] EWHC 1256 (QB) where, in the absence of supporting documentary evidence, £500 was allowed in respect of a claim for past medication in the sum of £750));

vi) a claim for losses where care was reasonably required as a result of the alleged negligence. This is rare in dental negligence cases, but can arise when, for example, a Claimant has been hospitalised following a bout of cellulitis and has needed to pay for care, or has required gratuitous care, in the recovery period.

2. Pain, Suffering and Loss of Amenity

The section of the Judicial College Guidelines which is most often relevant in dental negligence claims is, at present (in the 16th edition), Chapter 10 (A) (f),

> "*Damage to Teeth*
>
> *In these cases there will generally have been a course of treatment as a result of the initial injury. The amounts awarded will vary according to the extent and/or the degree of discomfort of such treatment. Any difficulty with eating increases the award. These cases may overlap with fractures of the jaw, meriting awards in the brackets for such fractures. Awards may be greater where the damage results in or is caused by protracted dentistry.*
>
> *Significant, chronic, tooth pain (such as from an untreated abscess) extending over a number of years together with significant general deterioration in the overall condition of teeth:*
>
> *Up to £38,130*
>
> *(i) Loss of or serious damage to several front teeth.*
>
> *£8,730 to £11,410*
>
> *(ii) Loss of or serious damage to two front teeth. The loss of two front teeth will attract an award in the middle to upper end of this bracket and damage to two front teeth or loss of two milk teeth will attract an award at the lower end.*

£4,350 to £7,630

(iii) Loss of or serious damage to one front tooth.

£2,200 to £3,950

(iv) Loss of or damage to back teeth: per tooth:

£1,090 to £1,710"

Note that whilst the figure for loss or damage to individual teeth is relatively low, the award can be higher where there have been losses as a result of protracted dentistry, or where chronic tooth pain has extended over a number of years along with significant general deterioration of the overall condition of the teeth. This is relevant, for example, when there has been alleged negligence over a period of many years. Case law is helpful in these cases when assessing what it might be reasonable for a Claimant to expect to receive.

3. Future Losses

These losses will include the anticipated future treatment costs to remedy the losses caused by the alleged negligence, the anticipated travel costs for such treatment, and also the maintenance costs following such treatment (for example, experts usually include a figure for maintenance of implants, and also, a figure for replacement of restorations at regular intervals).

When calculating future losses it is, of course, important to utilise the Ogden tables.

The Defendant may well put forward a lower figure for future losses depending on what their expert feels is reasonable in terms of future treatment costs, and whether it is their opinion that treatment can be obtained at a lower cost than what the Claimant proposes. There can also be arguments over whether the Claimant is a suitable candidate for the future treatment proposed. For example, a Claimant may seek implants, but a Defendant may raise the argument that they are not an appropriate candidate for implants due to inability to maintain good oral hygiene, or due to smoking. The option of dentures would then be able to be provided at a much lower cost than implants, and it would be for the parties (or the court) to decide whether it is likely that the Claimant, in this example, would be able to improve their oral hygiene and stop smoking such that implants would be a reasonable treatment option.

The Claimant should also consider whether there is likely to be any future loss of earnings whilst undergoing the future treatment proposed / recovering from surgery and in very rare cases, whether care is likely to be required.

CHAPTER EIGHT

NON-DELEGABLE DUTY OF CARE AND VICARIOUS LIABILITY IN DENTAL NEGLIGENCE CASES

An associate dentist is usually labelled as being self-employed, and this status is recognised as such by HMRC.

Whether a practice principal or limited company owes patients of the practice a non-delegable duty of care, and whether a practice principal or limited company is vicariously liable for the actions and omissions of their associates, is something that the courts have grappled with recently. There are several notable cases, one of these cases having reached the Court of Appeal in 2022, and the development of the recent case law in this area is set out in this Chapter, with some takeaway points at the end.

In 2014, His Honour Judge Richard Seymour QC as he then was, sitting as a judge of the High Court, considered the issue of vicarious liability in the case of *Whetstone v Medical Protection Society Limited* [2014] EWHC 1024 (QB) which involved alleged dental negligence on the part of an associate. The judge found that the the Defendant was vicariously liable for the acts and omissions of his associate due to the very close control which the Defendant had over his associate, including setting the associate's fees, providing equipment and staff. Further, his associate was unable to take patients or records with him were he to leave. The relationship was described as being "*as 'akin to employment' as one could get in a relationship deliberately structured by contract to avoid an employment relationship*".

Submissions were made to the effect that the principal may owe patients of the Practice a non-delegable duty, but this was not pleaded and therefore could not be considered on this occasion.

There followed three cases in 2020 and 2021 which considered the issue of non-delegable duty of care and vicarious liability in dental negligence claims, *Ramdhean v (1) Agedo and (2) The Forum Dental Practice Ltd* [2020] 1 WLUK 406, *Breakingbury v Croad* (unreported) 2021 and *Hughes v Rattan* [2021] EWHC 2032 (QB).

In *Ramdhean*, it was found that The Forum Dental Practice Ltd (the Second Defendant) owed the Claimant, a patient of the Practice, a non-delegable duty of care and was also vicariously liable for the actions of their associates.

With regard to non-delegable duty of care, the judge in *Ramdhean* (Her Honour Judge Belcher) applied the judgment in the Supreme Court case of *Woodland v Essex County Council* [2013] UKSC 66 where Lord Sumption comprehensively reviewed existing case law and identified five "defining features" which give rise to a non-delegable duty of care [paragraph 23]:

"

> *(1) The claimant is a patient or a child, or for some other reason is especially vulnerable or dependent on the protection of the defendant against the risk of injury. Other examples are likely to be prisoners and residents in care homes.*
>
> *(2) There is an antecedent relationship between the claimant and the defendant, independent of the negligent act or omission itself, (i) which places the claimant in the actual custody, charge or care of the defendant, and (ii) from which it is possible to impute to the defendant the*

assumption of a positive duty to protect the claimant from harm, and not just a duty to refrain from conduct which will foreseeably damage the claimant. It is characteristic of such relationships that they involve an element of control over the claimant, which varies in intensity from one situation to another, but is clearly very substantial in the case of schoolchildren.

(3) *The claimant has no control over how the defendant chooses to perform those obligations, i.e. whether personally or through employees or through third parties.*

(4) *The defendant has delegated to a third party some function which is an integral part of the positive duty which he has assumed towards the claimant; and the third party is exercising, for the purpose of the function thus delegated to him, the defendant's custody or care of the claimant and the element of control that goes with it.*

(5) *The third party has been negligent not in some collateral respect but in the performance of the very function assumed by the defendant and delegated by the defendant to him."*

It was found that the five *Woodland* characteristics applied, and that it was fair, just and reasonable to impose the higher duty of care which results in the imposition of a non-delegable duty.

Having found that a non-delegable duty of care existed, HHJ Belcher made it clear that it was unnecessary to go on to consider the alternative issue as to whether vicarious liability applied, but felt it necessary to do so in any event.

It was found, *obiter*, that The Forum Dental Practice Ltd was vicariously liable for the actions and omissions of its associates, HHJ

Belcher considering the two questions as set out in paragraph 2 of Lord Reed's judgment in *Cox v Ministry of Justice* [2016] UKSC 10,

> "*First, what sort of relationship has to exist between an individual and a defendant before the defendant can be made vicariously liable in tort for the conduct of that individual?*
>
> *Secondly, in what manner does the conduct of that individual have to be related to that relationship, in order for vicarious liability to be imposed on the defendant?*"

and the five criteria identified by Lord Phillips at paragraph 35 of *The Catholic Child Welfare Society v The Institute of the Brothers of the Christian Schools* [2012] UKSC 56:

> "*The relationship that gives rise to vicarious liability is in the vast majority of cases that of employer and employee under a contract of employment. The employer will be vicariously liable when the employee commits a tort in the course of his employment. There is no difficulty in identifying a number of policy reasons that usually make it fair, just and reasonable to impose vicarious liability on the employer when these criteria are satisfied:*
>
> *i) The employer is more likely to have the means to compensate the victim than the employee and can be expected to have insured against that liability;*
>
> *ii) The tort will have been committed as a result of activity being taken by the employee on behalf of the employer;*
>
> *iii) The employee's activity is likely to be part of the business activity of the employer;*

> *iv) The employer, by employing the employee to carry on the activity will have created the risk of the tort committed by the employee;*
>
> *v) The employee will, to a greater or lesser degree, have been under the control of the employer."*

At the time of *Ramdhean*, whilst *Barclays Bank plc v Various Claimants* [2018] EWCA Civ 1760 had been the subject of an appeal to the Supreme Court, and the matter had been heard, judgment had not yet been handed down.

In *Breakingbury*, the Claimant argued that the Defendant, a dental practice owner, owed a non-delegable duty of care to her as a patient of the practice (regardless of whether he personally treated her), and also that the Defendant could be held vicariously liable for the negligent treatment of her by an associate dentist who worked within his practice. The Claimant was successful on both points.

With regard to the issue of non-delegable duty of care, the judge (His Honour Judge Harrison), like HHJ Blecher in *Ramdhean*, considered the five defining features identified in *Woodland.* Having found that they had been met, he also found that it was right to impose a non-delegable duty in the case (stating, at paragraph 48, that the Defendant may well be entitled to an indemnity from individual associates, and that may go some way to dealing with any perceived unfairness).

Like HHJ Belcher in *Ramdhean*, having found that a non-delegable duty of care existed, HHJ Harrison said that it was perhaps not necessary to consider the issue of vicarious liability, but went on to consider it in any event. Judgment had, when *Breakingbury* was heard, been handed down in the case of *Various Claimants v Barclays Bank* [2020] UKSC 13 and HHJ Harrison considered and applied this in his judgment. In *Barclays Bank*, Lady Hale, with whom Lord Reed,

Lord Kerr, Lord Hodge and Lord Lloyd-Jones agreed, had considered five policy reasons as to why the imposition of vicarious liability might be fair, just and reasonable as identified by Lord Phillips in the *Christian Brothers Case.* HHJ Harrison in *Breakingbury* identified that it had been emphasised by Lady Hale in *Barclays Bank* that these policy reasons were not "*some sort of checklist*" [paragraph 55, *Breakingbury*]. What was said by Lady Hale at paragraph 1 of *Barclays Bank* is as follows,

> "*Two elements have to be shown before one person can be made vicariously liable for the torts committed by another. The first is a relationship between the two persons which makes it proper for the law to make the one pay for the fault of the other. Historically, and leaving aside relationships such as agency and partnership, that was limited to the relationship between employer and employee, but that has now been somewhat broadened…The second is the connection between that relationship and the tortfeasor's wrongdoing.*"

At paragraph 27, Lady Hale stated the following,

> "*The question therefore is, as it has always been, whether the tortfeasor is carrying on business on his own account or whether he is in a relationship akin to employment with the defendant. In doubtful cases, the five "incidents" identified by Lord Phillips may be helpful in identifying a relationship which is sufficiently analogous to employment to make it fair, just and reasonable to impose vicarious liability…Where it is clear that the tortfeasor is carrying on his own independent business it is not necessary to consider the five incidents.*"

HHJ Harrison found in *Breakingbury* that the practice was the provider of dental care, and that the practice had an overarching obligation to ensure that the dental services provided were safe and met the expected standard. He found that there was sufficient control to establish vicarious liability, particularly with regard to (among other matters) the setting of targets by the practice which was, in his judgment, telling the associates what they were required to do. He found that this sort of control was sufficient to form the basis of vicarious liability and was "akin to employment", and also found that the fact that associates managed their own tax affairs and/or made their own insurance arrangements did not displace that conclusion. He also noted that his findings were in keeping with HHJ Belcher in the *Ramdhean* case.

Hughes concerned the alleged dental negligence of four associates within the Practice at the material time, three of whom were self-employed and the fourth employed as a vocational trainee. Having sold it in March 2015, the Defendant, Mr Rattan, had owned the Practice for twenty eight years. During the period that the Claimant had received treatment, the Defendant was the sole principal dentist, but did not personally treat the Claimant at any stage.

Heather Williams QC as she then was, sitting as a deputy High Court Judge, found on a trial of the preliminary issues in *Hughes* that the Defendant owed the Claimant a non-delegable duty of care, and was vicariously liable for the actions and omissions of his associates.

With regard to non-delegable duty of care, she considered the five defining features identified in *Woodland.* She considered the first three factors in great detail and found that they applied. Counsel for the Defendant had already conceded that, if the Claimant could establish that the first three applied, then the fourth and fifth factors would also be present. Thus, it was concluded that the Defendant owed a non-delegable duty of care to the Claimant in relation to the dental treatment that she received at the Practice. Heather Williams QC stated that, in light of the above, it was not necessary for her to consider vicarious liability but considered it appropriate to do so in any event.

Applying the Supreme Court decision in *Barclays Bank*, Heather Williams QC concluded *obiter* that the relationship between the Defendant and the associate dentists was sufficiently akin to employment to make it fair and just to hold the former responsible for their acts and omissions, and to impose vicarious liability. She made this decision by considering several factors which she said demonstrated that a sufficient degree of control was present in respect of the Defendant and the associate dentists, and also several factors which she said demonstrated that the associate dentists were providing dental treatment as an integral part of the Defendant's dental practice, as opposed to them working as part of their own independent businesses. The Defendant conceded that, if this first relationship criterion was met, then the second limb of the *Barclays* test, concerning the closeness of the connection between the relationship and the alleged wrongdoing, was satisfied. Thus, the judge concluded, *obiter*, that the Defendant was vicariously liable for the acts and omissions of the four associates in respect of the Claimant's dental treatment at the Practice.

The decision in *Hughes* was appealed to the Court of Appeal and judgment handed down in 2022: *Hughes v Rattan* [2022] EWCA Civ 107. Lord Justice Bean (Lady Justice Nicola Davies and Lady Justice Simler assenting) stated in paragraphs [68 – 72] that he considered that the High Court was right to hold that the Defendant owed a non-delegable duty of care to the Claimant and that she was a patient of the Defendant's practice, not just in layman's language but as a matter of law. He found this for several reasons, the first of which was relying upon the Personal Dental Treatment Plan signed by the Claimant which named the Defendant as the Provider of the treatment, the second being the terms and restrictive covenants in the implied associate agreement based on a standard template British Dental

Association ("BDA") contract, and thirdly he found that the High Court was right to find that the Claimant satisfied all of the factors identified by Lord Sumption at paragraph [23] of *Woodland.*

Lord Justice Bean considered that the first factor did not require that the Claimant had to be within a subset of especially vulnerable patients in order to qualify. The word "patient" must include anyone receiving treatment from a dentist (but note, it was said that whether it includes medical or dental patients who are not actually subjected to treatment, but merely advised in consultation, is a question for another case and another day).

Turning to the second factor, it was stated that an antecedent relationship between the Claimant and Defendant was established at the latest on each occasion when Claimant signed the Personal Dental Treatment Plan, which she was required to do before any NHS treatment was carried out. That relationship placed the Claimant in the actual care of the Defendant, not because he was a dentist himself, but because he was the owner of the Practice, and involved an element of control.

As for the third factor, it was found that the Claimant had no control over how the Defendant chose to perform his obligations, whether personally or through employees or third parties. She could express a preference as to which associate dentist she would like to treat her, or could refuse treatment, but that would be no different to any patient with full capacity.

There was no issue with regard to the fourth and fifth factors given that the Defendant had conceded that if the first three factors had been satisfied then they need not be considered.

However, Lord Justice Bean (Lady Justice Nicola Davies and Lady Justice Simler assenting) concluded that the principal Mr Rattan was **not**, in fact, vicariously liable for the actions of his associates.

With regard to vicarious liability, Lord Justice Bean considered that the *Barclays* test for vicarious liability (clarified as being whether the alleged tortfeasor's relationship with the defendant can properly be described as being "akin" to employment, this time with the focus being on the contractual arrangements between tortfeasor and defendant) was not met.

Thus, the Defendant was not found to be vicariously liable for the acts or omissions of his associate dentists. Lord Justice Bean found this for several reasons as follows, the first two of which he said were the most significant (at [89]):

> "*(1) The Associate Dentists were free to work at the Practice for as many or as few hours as they wished;*
>
> *(2) They were also free to work for other practice owners and businesses, and some in fact did so;*
>
> *(3) The Defendant had no right to control, and did not control, the clinical judgments they made or the way in which they carried out treatment;*
>
> *(4) They chose which laboratories to use and shared the cost of disbursements to laboratories;*
>
> *(5) They were responsible for their own tax and national insurance payments, and were treated as independent contractors by HMRC;*

(6) *Although the Defendant took most of the financial risk by virtue of running the premises and paying ancillary staff, they shared the risk of bad debts;*

(7) *They were required to carry personal professional indemnity insurance and to indemnify the Defendant against any claims made against him in respect of their treatment of patients;*

(8) *They had to pay for their own professional clothing and professional development, and for any equipment they wished to use which was not provided by the Practice;*

(9) *There was no disciplinary or grievance procedure.*"

He took into account factors which pointed the other way as follows: he said at paragraph [90] that the Defendant (practice principal) decided on the opening hours of the Practice and provided equipment and facilities, and he had a limited degree of control in that he was under a duty to the NHS to ensure that courses of treatment were completed within a reasonable period of time. He also considered that the associate dentists were under a contractual duty to follow the policies and procedures of the Practice (however, it did not appear that there were in fact any such policies or procedures which were relevant to show control).

On balance, however, he did not consider that these indicators outweighed the nine factors mentioned in [89] and set out above so as to make the relationship sufficiently analogous to employment to satisfy the *Barclays* test.

It was also considered that the label "licence fee" in relation to the 50% of fees for NHS treatment retained by the Practice was wholly artificial, and whether associate dentists were "workers" was irrelevant.

In this case, there was no written agreement between Mr Rattan and his associates, and the British Dental Association standard template was implied.

It is worth noting that *Hughes* could yet be appealed to the Supreme Court, but at the time of writing, it is binding on lower courts.

Takeaway points

The decisions in *Ramdhean*, *Brakingbury* and *Hughes* have been consistent in finding that a practice principal, or limited company, owes the patient of the practice a non-delegable duty of care by applying the five defining features in *Woodland*. Each case was decided on the facts, but following the application of the law to these cases, it is likely that, in circumstances where a practice operates similarly to a practice in one of these cases, a court would make a similar finding. Thus, should there be a potential dental negligence claim where the treating dentist at the material time cannot be traced or is not properly indemnified, then bringing a non-delegable duty of care claim against the practice principal or limited company is a way to help ensure that the Claimant is not left without a remedy.

In all three cases, vicarious liability was found to apply at first instance. However, the practice principal was not found to be vicariously liable for the actions of their associates in the Court of Appeal in the case of *Hughes*. This decision was made on the facts, therefore it would be necessary to consider the factors taken into account by Lord Justice Bean when assessing the likelihood of success of such a claim. Of course, this will be easier for the Defendant to assess at the outset as opposed to the Claimant given that the Claimant is unlikely to have a great deal of knowledge as to how the practice operates when intending to bring a claim.

It is worth bearing in mind, however, that not all indemnifiers are providing their members with back-dated insurance for non-delegable duty of care and vicarious liability claims, and so there is always a risk that the Claimant may not be able to recover all of their damages and costs in such a claim.

CHAPTER NINE

PROCEDURAL MATTERS IN DENTAL NEGLIGENCE CASES

Pre-Action Procedure

I don't intend to delve too deeply into general procedural issues as information on that topic is covered in other books, and the focus of this book is intended to give the reader important tips for dental negligence cases. Therefore, I pick a case example up at the point at which the Letter of Claim is drafted following receipt of a positive breach and causation report.

The Letter of Claim is an important document which sets out the Claimant's case. See the Pre-Action Protocol for the Resolution of Clinical Disputes; the following sections below are particularly relevant:

> *"Letter of Claim*
>
> *1.3 It is important that each party to a clinical dispute has sufficient information and understanding of the other's perspective and case to be able to investigate a claim efficiently and, where appropriate, to resolve it. This Protocol encourages a cards-on-the-table approach when something has gone wrong with a claimant's treatment or the claimant is dissatisfied with that treatment and/or the outcome.*

3.14 If, following the receipt and analysis of the records, and the receipt of any further advice (including from experts if necessary – see Section 4), the claimant decides that there are grounds for a claim, a letter of claim should be sent to the defendant as soon as practicable. Any letter of claim sent to an NHS Trust should be copied to the National Health Service Litigation Authority.

3.16 This letter should contain—

(a) a clear summary of the facts on which the claim is based, including the alleged adverse outcome, and the main allegations of negligence;

(b) a description of the claimant's injuries, and present condition and prognosis;

(c) an outline of the financial loss incurred by the claimant, with an indication of the heads of damage to be claimed and the scale of the loss, unless this is impracticable;

(d) confirmation of the method of funding and whether any funding arrangement was entered into before or after April 2013; and

(e) the discipline of any expert from whom evidence has already been obtained.

3.17 The Letter of Claim should refer to any relevant documents, including health records, and if possible enclose copies of any of those which will not already be in the potential defendant's possession, e.g. any relevant general practitioner records if the claimant's claim is against a hospital.

> *3.18 Sufficient information must be given to enable the defendant to focus investigations and to put an initial valuation on the claim.*
>
> *3.19 Letters of Claim are not intended to have the same formal status as Particulars of Claim, nor should any sanctions necessarily apply if the Letter of Claim and any subsequent Particulars of Claim in the proceedings differ."*

In the Letter of Claim, the Claimant should set out the chronology, alleged breaches, causation and loss with sufficient clarity for the Defendant to be able to properly consider the case, but it need not be as fully particularised as the Particulars of Claim will be. A template is included in Annex C2 to the Protocol.

The Letter of Claim can be drafted by a solicitor, or counsel may be instructed to consider the expert evidence and draft the Letter of Claim, with or without a conference with the expert as necessary. Should the Claimant wish to put forward a Part 36 Offer at this stage, then it would be wise to first instruct counsel to advise on quantum. Paragraph 3.21 describes the steps that ought to be taken in putting forward an offer at this stage:

> "*3.21 The claimant may want to make an offer to settle the claim at this early stage by putting forward an offer in respect of liability and/or an amount of compensation in accordance with the legal and procedural requirements of CPR Part 36 (possibly including any costs incurred to date). If an offer to settle is made, generally this should be supported by a medical report which deals with the injuries, condition and prognosis, and by a schedule of loss and supporting documentation. The level of detail necessary will depend on the value of the claim. Medical reports may not be*

necessary where there is no significant continuing injury and a detailed schedule may not be necessary in a low value case."

Upon receipt of the Letter of Claim, the Defendant should consider the case and, following an expert review of the case, draft an appropriate Letter of Response with admissions and denials as necessary so as to narrow the issues. Relevant paragraphs from the Pre-Action Protocol are set out below:

"Letter of Response

3.23 The defendant should acknowledge the Letter of Claim within 14 days of receipt and should identify who will be dealing with the matter.

3.24 The defendant should, within four months of the Letter of Claim, provide a reasoned answer in the form of a Letter of Response in which the defendant should—

(a) if the claim is admitted, say so in clear terms;

(b) if only part of the claim is admitted, make clear which issues of breach of duty and/or causation are admitted and which are denied and why;

(c) state whether it is intended that any admissions will be binding;

(d) if the claim is denied, include specific comments on the allegations of negligence and, if a synopsis or chronology of relevant events has been provided and is disputed, the defendant's version of those events;

(e) *if supportive expert evidence has been obtained, identify which disciplines of expert evidence have been relied upon and whether they relate to breach of duty and/or causation;*

(f) *if known, state whether the defendant requires copies of any relevant medical records obtained by the claimant (to be supplied for a reasonable copying charge);*

(g) *provide copies of any additional documents relied upon, e.g. an internal protocol;*

(h) *if not indemnified by the NHS, supply details of the relevant indemnity insurer; and*

(i) *inform the claimant of any other potential defendants to the claim.*

3.25

3.25.1 If the defendant requires an extension of time for service of the Letter of Response, a request should be made as soon as the defendant becomes aware that it will be required and, in any event, within four months of the letter of claim.

3.25.2 The defendant should explain why any extension of time is necessary.

3.25.3 The claimant should adopt a reasonable approach to any request for an extension of time for provision of the reasoned answer."

A template Letter of Response can be found at Annex C3 of the Pre-Action Protocol.

Paragraph 3.26 sets out how a Defendant should respond to a Part 36 Offer made by the Claimant, and what should be provided should the Defendant wish to make a Part 36 Offer:

> "*3.26 If the claimant has made an offer to settle, the defendant should respond to that offer in the Letter of Response, preferably with reasons. The defendant may also make an offer to settle at this stage. Any offer made by the defendant should be made in accordance with the legal and procedural requirements of CPR Part 36 (possibly including any costs incurred to date). If an offer to settle is made, the defendant should provide sufficient medical or other evidence to allow the claimant to properly consider the offer. The level of detail necessary will depend on the value of the claim.*"

Upon receipt of the Letter of Response, it is likely that negotiations will take place and an attempt be made to settle the claim if at all possible. The Pre-Action Protocol provides guidance as to how this ought to proceed:

> "*3.27 If the parties reach agreement on liability, or wish to explore the possibility of resolution with no admissions as to liability, but time is needed to resolve the value of the claim, they should aim to agree a reasonable period.*
>
> *3.28 If the parties do not reach agreement on liability, they should discuss whether the claimant should start proceedings and whether the court might be invited to direct an early trial of a preliminary issue or of breach of duty and/or causation.*

> *3.29 Following receipt of the Letter of Response, if the claimant is aware that there may be a delay of six months or more before the claimant decides if, when and how to proceed, the claimant should keep the defendant generally informed."*

Should it be the case that negotiations do not result in a settlement being reached, then both parties need to consider whether they feel that their case is strong enough to run. Note that the Pre-Action Protocol advises parties to consider the possibility of settling the claim through Alternative Dispute Resolution at all stages.

See paragraph 3.20 of the Pre-action Protocol:

> "***3.20*** *Proceedings should not be issued until after four months from the letter of claim. In certain instances it may not be possible for the claimant to serve a Letter of Claim more than four months before the expiry of the limitation period. If, for any reason, proceedings are started before the parties have complied, they should seek to agree to apply to the court for an order to stay the proceedings whilst the parties take steps to comply."*

The Conference

A conference should take place between solicitor, counsel, lay client and expert(s) before the Particulars of Claim are drafted. Likewise, a conference should take place between solicitor, counsel, expert(s) and the member before the Defence is drafted.

The Claimant

In preparation for the conference, counsel should have an understanding of the chronology and prepare a list of breach and causation points, as well as losses which flow from the alleged breaches.

If there is anything that is missing from the expert report or which needs to be further clarified, then this is the time to identify that and ask the expert to amend their report accordingly. An example is where the expert has said that there has been breach of duty in the way in which root canal therapy was carried out. It is important to know what, exactly, went wrong with this particular root canal treatment (for example, failure to properly obturate one of the canals), and this should be clearly set out in the report.

Where there are two or more experts instructed on behalf of the Claimant, and their opinions differ, then it is important before the Particulars of Claim are drafted that the experts discuss their opinions openly in conference so that the Claimant's case can be crystallised.

Having the lay client present is helpful in order to clarify certain points, for example, what the Claimant says was discussed when gaining consent, or what they understood treatment options to be and what they would have done had they been provided with alternative treatment options. This is, of course, necessary when considering causation in a consent case. The lay client can often shed further light onto what happened from their perspective.

Where any alleged breaches of duty have been denied by the Defendant in the Letter of Response, these denials should be put to the expert and the expert given the opportunity to respond and amend their report if necessary.

It is also important to challenge the expert on causation points in order to ensure that any alleged breaches are causative. If not, they are not relevant. Again, any causation points which are denied in the Letter of Response ought to be put to the expert so that they have the opportunity to respond and amend their report if necessary.

Should the Defendant challenge quantum as claimed, then the condition and prognosis expert for the Claimant ought to be given the opportunity to respond to such challenges.

The Defendant

In preparation for drafting the Defence, all allegations of breach of duty made in the Particulars of Claim should be put to the Defendant / treating clinician at the material time in conference, and a decision made to admit, deny or put the Claimant to proof in respect of each allegation. Where an allegation is denied, or where the Claimant is put to proof, a reason should be given. The expert who drafted the breach and causation report should also be asked to comment as to breach.

The breach and causation expert should also be invited to comment as to causation. Again, allegations of causation should be admitted, denied or the Claimant put to proof, and where an allegation is not admitted, a reason should be given.

Where the condition and prognosis expert puts forward alternative figures for quantum, these should be fully explored so that a counter-schedule can be drafted on behalf of the Defendant.

Issuing Proceedings

If all attempts at settlement have failed, and the Claimant decides to issue proceedings, then Civil Procedure Rules 16.2 and 16.3 apply, as well as Practice Direction 16.

Bear in mind that limitation is three years from the date on which the cause of action accrued; or the date of knowledge (if later) of the person injured (s11 Limitation Act 1980). Knowledge refers to the date on which the Claimant first had knowledge of the following facts: a) that the injury in question was significant; and (b) that the injury was attributable in whole or in part to the act or omission which is alleged to constitute negligence or breach of duty; and (c) the identity of the defendant; and (d) if it is alleged that the act or omission was that of a person other than the defendant, the identity of that person and the additional facts supporting the bringing of an action against the defendant (s14 Limitation Act 1980).

Following the conference, if no further evidence is required, counsel for the Claimant should be in a position to draft the Particulars of Claim. Civil Procedure Rule 16.4 and Practice Direction 16 apply; I don't intend to cover these in this book as they should be well known to legal practitioners. In the Particulars of Claim, the breaches of duty should be fully particularised, and causation in relation to the breaches clearly set out. The Condition and Prognosis Report(s) which the Claimant intends to rely upon should be served with the Particulars of Claim, as should a Schedule of Loss.

TOP TIP

As a starting point, once counsel has drafted the Particulars of Claim, it can be helpful (if Limitation allows) for a draft to be sent to the Defendant for consideration ahead of issuing proceedings. Both parties will then have a very clear idea of the Claimant's case, and can then reconsider their position and attempt to reach settlement.

When drafting the Defence, Civil Procedure Rules 16.5 and 16.6 apply, as does Practice Direction 16. Where the Defendant is relying upon their own medical evidence, the condition and prognosis report should be served with the Defence, as should a counter-schedule if quantum is disputed.

The Claimant may file a Reply to the Defence pursuant to CPR 16.7 should they feel it appropriate or necessary to do so.

There are no particular stand out features in dental negligence cases beyond this stage to trial procedurally when compared with other clinical negligence cases, and it is beyond the scope of this book to consider procedure in clinical negligence cases generally as this information can be found in other texts.

CHAPTER TEN

CONCLUSION

Whist dental negligence cases generally follow clinical negligence cases in terms of procedure and law, there are unique stand out features of dental negligence cases, examples of which are provided throughout this book, which mean that it is helpful to have some understanding of the subject in order to properly navigate through the litigation process.

It is hoped that the gentle introduction to terminology used in dental records, notes of challenges frequently faced in dental negligence cases and top tips throughout the book help to provide the reader with a feel for what it means to be a dental negligence lawyer. Further, the law considered in the consent and non-delegable duty of care / vicarious liability chapters aims to provide the reader with an understanding of relevant case law which often crops up in dental negligence cases.

The law is up to date at the time of writing, but ever changing, and it is hoped that the reader is inspired to get involved with cases in this fascinating, demanding and, at times, challenging area of law.

MORE BOOKS BY LAW BRIEF PUBLISHING

A selection of our other titles available now:-

'A Practical Guide to Parental Alienation in Private and Public Law Children Cases' by Sam King QC & Frankie Shama
'Contested Heritage – Removing Art from Land and Historic Buildings' by Richard Harwood QC, Catherine Dobson, David Sawtell
'The Limits of Separate Legal Personality: When Those Running a Company Can Be Held Personally Liable for Losses Caused to Third Parties Outside of the Company' by Dr Mike Wilkinson
'A Practical Guide to Transgender Law' by Robin Moira White & Nicola Newbegin
'Artificial Intelligence – The Practical Legal Issues (2nd Edition)' by John Buyers
'A Practical Guide to Residential Freehold Conveyancing' by Lorraine Richardson
'A Practical Guide to Pensions on Divorce for Lawyers' by Bryan Scant
'A Practical Guide to Challenging Sham Marriage Allegations in Immigration Law' by Priya Solanki
'A Practical Guide to Legal Rights in Scotland' by Sarah-Jane Macdonald
'A Practical Guide to New Build Conveyancing' by Paul Sams & Rebecca East
'A Practical Guide to Defending Barristers in Disciplinary Cases' by Marc Beaumont
'A Practical Guide to Inherited Wealth on Divorce' by Hayley Trim
'A Practical Guide to Practice Direction 12J and Domestic Abuse in Private Law Children Proceedings' by Rebecca Cross & Malvika Jaganmohan
'A Practical Guide to Confiscation and Restraint' by Narita Bahra QC, John Carl Townsend, David Winch
'A Practical Guide to the Law of Forests in Scotland' by Philip Buchan
'A Practical Guide to Health and Medical Cases in Immigration Law' by Rebecca Chapman & Miranda Butler
'A Practical Guide to Bad Character Evidence for Criminal Practitioners by Aparna Rao
'A Practical Guide to Extradition Law post-Brexit' by Myles Grandison et al

'A Practical Guide to Hoarding and Mental Health for Housing Lawyers' by Rachel Coyle
'A Practical Guide to Psychiatric Claims in Personal Injury – 2nd Edition' by Liam Ryan
'Stephens on Contractual Indemnities' by Richard Stephens
'A Practical Guide to the EU Succession Regulation' by Richard Frimston
'A Practical Guide to Solicitor and Client Costs – 2nd Edition' by Robin Dunne
'Constructive Dismissal – Practice Pointers and Principles' by Benjimin Burgher
'A Practical Guide to Religion and Belief Discrimination Claims in the Workplace' by Kashif Ali
'A Practical Guide to the Law of Medical Treatment Decisions' by Ben Troke
'Fundamental Dishonesty and QOCS in Personal Injury Proceedings: Law and Practice' by Jake Rowley
'A Practical Guide to the Law in Relation to School Exclusions' by Charlotte Hadfield & Alice de Coverley
'A Practical Guide to Divorce for the Silver Separators' by Karin Walker
'The Right to be Forgotten – The Law and Practical Issues' by Melissa Stock
'A Practical Guide to Planning Law and Rights of Way in National Parks, the Broads and AONBs' by James Maurici QC, James Neill et al
'A Practical Guide to Election Law' by Tom Tabori
'A Practical Guide to the Law in Relation to Surrogacy' by Andrew Powell
'A Practical Guide to Claims Arising from Fatal Accidents – 2nd Edition' by James Patience
'A Practical Guide to the Ownership of Employee Inventions – From Entitlement to Compensation' by James Tumbridge & Ashley Roughton
'A Practical Guide to Asbestos Claims' by Jonathan Owen & Gareth McAloon
'A Practical Guide to Stamp Duty Land Tax in England and Northern Ireland' by Suzanne O'Hara
'A Practical Guide to the Law of Farming Partnerships' by Philip Whitcomb
'Covid-19, Homeworking and the Law – The Essential Guide to Employment and GDPR Issues' by Forbes Solicitors
'Covid-19 and Criminal Law – The Essential Guide' by Ramya Nagesh
'Covid-19 and Family Law in England and Wales – The Essential Guide' by Safda Mahmood

'A Practical Guide to the Law of Unlawful Eviction and Harassment – 2nd Edition' by Stephanie Lovegrove
'Covid-19, Brexit and the Law of Commercial Leases – The Essential Guide' by Mark Shelton
'A Practical Guide to Costs in Personal Injury Claims – 2nd Edition' by Matthew Hoe
'A Practical Guide to the General Data Protection Regulation (GDPR) – 2nd Edition' by Keith Markham
'Ellis on Credit Hire – Sixth Edition' by Aidan Ellis & Tim Kevan
'A Practical Guide to Working with Litigants in Person and McKenzie Friends in Family Cases' by Stuart Barlow
'Protecting Unregistered Brands: A Practical Guide to the Law of Passing Off' by Lorna Brazell
'A Practical Guide to Secondary Liability and Joint Enterprise Post-Jogee' by Joanne Cecil & James Mehigan
'A Practical Guide to the Pre-Action RTA Claims Protocol for Personal Injury Lawyers' by Antonia Ford
'A Practical Guide to Neighbour Disputes and the Law' by Alexander Walsh
'A Practical Guide to Forfeiture of Leases' by Mark Shelton
'A Practical Guide to Coercive Control for Legal Practitioners and Victims' by Rachel Horman
'A Practical Guide to Rights Over Airspace and Subsoil' by Daniel Gatty
'Tackling Disclosure in the Criminal Courts – A Practitioner's Guide' by Narita Bahra QC & Don Ramble
'A Practical Guide to the Law of Driverless Cars – Second Edition' by Alex Glassbrook, Emma Northey & Scarlett Milligan
'A Practical Guide to TOLATA Claims' by Greg Williams
'A Practical Guide to Elderly Law – 2nd Edition' by Justin Patten
'A Practical Guide to Responding to Housing Disrepair and Unfitness Claims' by Iain Wightwick
'A Practical Guide to the Construction and Rectification of Wills and Trust Instruments' by Edward Hewitt
'A Practical Guide to the Law of Bullying and Harassment in the Workplace' by Philip Hyland
'How to Be a Freelance Solicitor: A Practical Guide to the SRA-Regulated Freelance Solicitor Model' by Paul Bennett

'A Practical Guide to Prison Injury Claims' by Malcolm Johnson
'A Practical Guide to the Small Claims Track - 2nd Edition' by Dominic Bright
'A Practical Guide to Advising Clients at the Police Station' by Colin Stephen McKeown-Beaumont
'A Practical Guide to Antisocial Behaviour Injunctions' by Iain Wightwick
'Practical Mediation: A Guide for Mediators, Advocates, Advisers, Lawyers, and Students in Civil, Commercial, Business, Property, Workplace, and Employment Cases' by Jonathan Dingle with John Sephton
'The Mini-Pupillage Workbook' by David Boyle
'A Practical Guide to Crofting Law' by Brian Inkster
'A Practical Guide to Spousal Maintenance' by Liz Cowell
'A Practical Guide to the Law of Domain Names and Cybersquatting' by Andrew Clemson
'A Practical Guide to the Law of Gender Pay Gap Reporting' by Harini Iyengar
'A Practical Guide to the Rights of Grandparents in Children Proceedings' by Stuart Barlow
'NHS Whistleblowing and the Law' by Joseph England
'Employment Law and the Gig Economy' by Nigel Mackay & Annie Powell
'A Practical Guide to Noise Induced Hearing Loss (NIHL) Claims' by Andrew Mckie, Ian Skeate, Gareth McAloon
'An Introduction to Beauty Negligence Claims – A Practical Guide for the Personal Injury Practitioner' by Greg Almond
'Intercompany Agreements for Transfer Pricing Compliance' by Paul Sutton
'Zen and the Art of Mediation' by Martin Plowman
'A Practical Guide to the SRA Principles, Individual and Law Firm Codes of Conduct 2019 – What Every Law Firm Needs to Know' by Paul Bennett
'A Practical Guide to Adoption for Family Lawyers' by Graham Pegg
'A Practical Guide to Industrial Disease Claims' by Andrew Mckie & Ian Skeate
'A Practical Guide to Redundancy' by Philip Hyland
'A Practical Guide to Vicarious Liability' by Mariel Irvine
'A Practical Guide to Applications for Landlord's Consent and Variation of Leases' by Mark Shelton
'A Practical Guide to Relief from Sanctions Post-Mitchell and Denton' by Peter Causton

www.ingramcontent.com/pod-product-compliance
Ingram Content Group UK Ltd.
Pitfield, Milton Keynes, MK11 3LW, UK
UKHW020150290926
15471UKWH00004B/798

9 781914 608681